The Reading Comprehension Idea Book

Anthony D. Fredericks, Ed.D.
Reading Specialist
Catasauqua Area School District
Catasauqua, Pennsylvania

Scott, Foresman and Company
Glenview, Illinois
Dallas, Texas   Oakland, New Jersey   Palo Alto,
California   Tucker, Georgia   London

Dedication

To all the teachers and students at Sheckler Elementary School
who were the inspiration and motivation for the creation
of this book.

ISBN 0-673-15950-7

1 2 3 4 5 6 MAL 89 88 87 86 85 84

Preface

Elementary school teachers are aware that reading instruction involves more than just teaching decoding skills. Helping students comprehend written material is also a crucial objective of teaching reading. In addition, effective reading development should give children the opportunity to utilize their reading skills in meaningful, real-life activities. As a result, teachers are constantly on the lookout for materials and ideas that will help pupils develop their comprehension abilities beyond the pages of the basal text as well as broaden their reading experiences through a range of projects.

This book contains a wide variety of activities and ideas designed to get children *actively involved* in comprehending written material. An additional purpose of the book is to encourage the development of divergent thinking strategies, rather than promoting the right-answer syndrome commonly associated with comprehension workbooks.

The activities are organized around four reading skills that teachers consider essential to comprehension competence: getting the main idea, understanding sequence, grasping details, and drawing inferences. Each of the activities in this book has been successfully used in a number of elementary classrooms. They have been drawn from the daily living experiences of children and thus are motivational as well as instructional. The fact that pupils' personal experiences are integrated into these activities makes the associated reading instruction relevant and enhances the potential for comprehension development.

These activities, which focus on the processes appropriate for comprehension development and growth, are geared for a wide range of grades and pupil abilities. Individual teachers, who know their students best, will be able to choose age-appropriate projects to meet the specific reading levels and needs of their class. Adaptations included with each activity permit teachers to utilize these suggestions over a broad spectrum of pupils, talents, and grades. Thus, these ideas can be useful for remedial, so-called average, or gifted groups of students—a factor that permits teachers to introduce individual activities to meet a variety of needs or learning situations.

It is important, however, that, whatever activities you as a teacher choose, you take sufficient time to discuss the purpose of each project. Students must understand the relevance of specific activities to their regular classroom reading work, both in terms of comprehension skill development and overall literacy training. Alerting pupils to the fact that these projects are an extension of many everyday activities should be part of any preliminary discussions.

Although these activities are designed for a broad range of students and abilities, I encourage you to solicit personal adaptations or extra follow-up ideas from your class. When students have the opportunity to work with events most familiar to them, then they will be eager to participate actively in the learning experience. Students who have the opportunity to create, design, decorate, and set up these projects will be motivated to learn from them and stimulated to transfer this knowledge to a wide variety of reading experiences.

I also urge you to follow up each activity with a class, group, or individual discussion session. Merely dropping these projects into the reading curriculum will do little to advance individual reading development for pupils. Students must be able to understand the relationship of these suggestions to their own lives as well as to their own literacy growth. Discussions also have the advantage of providing you with an opportunity to focus on specific weaknesses or strengths, in the activities themselves as well as in students.

The activities have been designed so that you may choose to use them for individual instruction, small- or large-group work, or a whole-class learning experience. This option allows you the opportunity to select appropriate activities according to the specific dynamics of your classroom. In addition, feel free to pick and choose activities in any order you feel necessary. There is no set sequence for any of the projects: each is complete in itself and may be used at whatever time or place you feel to be most appropriate. Individual activities may be presented in a variety of formats, a selection of grouping strategies, and a diversity of schedules.

This book has been written for the teacher who wishes to motivate, stimulate, and encourage his or her students toward greater comprehension competence. A liberal sprinkling of these activities throughout the reading curriculum can help in the development of successful readers and the promotion of reading as a worthwhile and enjoyable lifelong habit.

Grouping Formats

The following chart allows you to select comprehension activities that are most suitable to your individual grouping strategies and instructional plans. The activity numbers for each comprehension skill are listed according to their utility within an individual, small-group, large-group, or whole-class format.

For example, if you want to select an activity emphasizing the skill of *sequencing* for a *small group* of students, select an appropriate project number from the second box in the sequence row. If you want to present an *inference* activity to the *whole class*, then select an activity number from the fourth box in the inference row.

Skill	Activity Number			
	Individual	**Small Group***	**Large Group****	**Whole Class**
Getting the Main Idea	1, 9, 10, 11, 12, 13, 14, 16, 17, 18	1, 4, 5, 9, 11, 13, 14, 18	5, 6, 8, 19	2, 3, 6, 7, 8, 15, 17, 19
Understanding Sequence	1, 2, 3, 4, 5, 7, 8, 9, 10, 11, 15, 16	5, 6, 7, 9, 12, 13	6, 7, 12, 13	7, 14, 15, 16, 17, 18
Grasping Details	2, 3, 8, 11, 13	1, 3, 4, 5, 6, 10, 13, 16, 17	1, 3, 4, 5, 7, 14, 15, 16	3, 8, 9, 12, 14, 15
Drawing Inferences	2, 4, 5, 7, 9, 10, 12	2, 4, 5, 9, 11, 13, 14, 15	1, 8, 13, 15	1, 3, 6, 8, 10, 16

*Divide the class into groups of two to four students each.
**Divide the class into three or four sections.

Contents

Contents

3

Grasping Details 42

4

Drawing Inferences 61

Student Participation Charts 79

1

Getting the Main Idea

Helping students to discover the main idea of a story or reading selection is an important comprehension objective. Oftentimes students are asked to summarize the important details of a story in order to determine the theme or plot. Yet children are sometimes confused by the multitude of facts, characters, and settings that are interwoven throughout a particular story. Sifting through these details in an attempt to determine the main idea can be an overwhelming and difficult task. Many students have a tendency to isolate certain details or irrelevant facts and present them as a summarization of the story. The attempt of students to figure out the main idea is often a very frustrating experience for both the students and the teacher trying to help them.

There are, however, a variety of activities that teachers can use to promote the acquisition of this important reading skill. Many

times, teachers will use a series of graded paragraphs that require students to choose one of three possible titles. A more effective way can be to use activities drawn from the students' real world of reading. Materials such as TV schedules, newspapers, comic strips, and recipes can be valuable in teaching and reinforcing this skill. They demonstrate that determining main ideas is a process we use in everyday activities, from choosing TV shows on the basis of brief program descriptions to writing telegrams in a few words. The use of a number of these activities integrated with regular classroom instruction can help pupils to see the significance of this reading skill as well as utilize it in their everyday contacts with literature.

All Together Now

Materials: Cardboard, scissors, markers, envelopes

Group size: Individual, small group

On a piece of stiff cardboard, write in large letters the main idea of a short story. Turn the cardboard over, and draw lines that divide it into five or six jigsaw pieces. Write one important detail from the story in each section. Cut the puzzle apart along the lines and place the pieces in an envelope. Ask members of the class to read the short story. When they are done, have them take the puzzle out of the envelope and put it together, with the detail side up. Point out to them that an important detail from the story is noted on each piece. Have them turn the completed puzzle over and read the story's main idea on the back. Have students make additional puzzles for other stories.

_____ **Adaptation** _____

Ask younger pupils to bring in old or discarded jigsaw puzzles of no more than eight pieces each. After you have read a story to the class, lead a discussion in which important facts from the story are identified. Write them on the jigsaw pieces. The title of the story can then be written on the reverse side. Students may wish to start a collection of these story puzzles.

Picture That

Materials: Camera and film, box, index cards
Group size: Whole class

Take several photographs of various classroom activities (reading groups, morning arrival, recess, a class visitor). Place these photos in a brightly decorated box. Direct each of the pupils to pick one photo at random and to write a title for the picture on an index card. Post the titles and pictures in an appropriate place on the bulletin board. Ask class members to vote for their favorite title.

_____ **Adaptation** _____

Select three pictures from a discarded magazine and post these on the chalkboard or bulletin board. Lead a class discussion on the differences between the pictures. Based upon the characteristics of each picture, have the class decide on appropriate titles. You may wish to provide an assortment of old magazines to the class and have them choose the necessary pictures.

Got a Match?

Materials: Old workbooks, scissors, glue, tagboard

Group size: Whole class

Select three or four stories, each with an accompanying illustration, from an old basal workbook. Mount each of these illustrations on tagboard, and display them in the chalkboard tray. Read one of the stories to the class, and ask the students to identify the picture in the tray that matches the contents of the story.

Later, you may wish to mount a group of pictures and a group of stories separately on tagboard and cut them out. Then have the students match up the stories and illustrations.

_____ **Adaptation** _____

After the class has read several stories in the basal text, direct groups of students to design a main idea illustration for each story. Also ask them to provide two additional illustrations that have nothing to do with any story.

Display each group's three illustrations, and have the rest of the class match the correct picture with each selected story.

The Place to Be!

Materials: Tape recorder, blank tapes

Group size: Small group

Provide a group of students with a tape recorder and blank tape. Instruct them to go to another location in the school building (for example, library, custodian's room, nurse's office) and to record a description of that place on tape, not specifically identifying it. Ask several different groups to record descriptions of many school locations.

Set up a tape player and several of these tapes in a corner of your room. Instruct students to listen to each tape and to identify its precise location. After all students have had an opportunity to listen to the tapes, direct them to label each one with the name of the location described in the recording.

_____ **Adaptation** _____

Have the students suggest names of specific locations within the school. Record these horizontally on the chalkboard. Go around the room and ask each pupil to suggest a one-word description for one of the locations, which can then be written under each title. Encourage the class to think of at least ten words for each selected place. Later on you may wish to use these words for vocabulary practice.

Tune In

Materials: Record player or tape recorder, selected music

Group size: Small group, large group

Music is one way you can get your students interested in main ideas. Discuss with your pupils the titles of popular songs and whether or not the titles accurately reflect the lyrics of the songs. Talk about the vocabulary, melody, or tempo that may influence a title choice. Provide a record player or tape recorder and several different kinds of musical selections (pop, rock, country). Direct a group of students to listen to a particular selection and to provide a title for it. They may want to play a selection for the rest of the class and defend their choice of title. Initiate discussions about whether the words make it easier to provide titles or whether mood and tempo have an effect. Compare the students' titles with the actual song titles.

―――― **Adaptation** ――――――――――――――――――――

For younger students, record a selection of familiar songs, lullabies, or nursery rhymes. Write the names of these selections on the chalkboard. Choose one recording at random, and play it for the class or group, asking the students to locate the appropriate title. Be sure to follow up with a discussion on why each title is specific to only a particular selection.

Photo-Graphic Minds

Materials: Magazines, index cards, camera and film

Group size: Large group, whole class

Help your students improve their ability to summarize all the details of a story by using pictures. Have your students pretend that they are directors of a museum and that several new pictures have arrived at the museum without their titles. Display several magazine pictures on the bulletin board. Have students write down appropriate titles on index cards and tack them under each picture. Then have the entire class decide on the best title for each picture. You may also want to take photographs of some class activities and post these on the bulletin board. Direct your students to provide titles for these as well.

_____ Adaptation _____

Ask several students to bring in photos from home. These can be displayed for the entire class (try to choose photos that show some action). After several days, you may wish to select several of these photos and lead a class discussion on titles that may be appropriate for each one. This could also be an ongoing activity, with one photo selected as picture of the week and the entire class deciding an appropriate title.

Class Calendar

Materials: Large desk or wall calendar

Group size: Whole class

Provide practice in summarizing details through the use of a class calendar. At the end of each school day, ask several students to tell about some of that day's significant events (not just everyday events such as lunch or recess). Then ask the class members to suggest a title for the day. Write these daily titles on a large class calendar and keep a record of your activities for the year. For example:

October 20—*Mysterious Happenings*

1. The world globe is missing.

2. Five police cars go by the school.

3. The water fountain doesn't work.

—————— **Adaptation** ———————————————————————

You may wish to provide each student with a photocopied sheet listing the days of the week. Lead a class discussion on the events or activities of the day that students can record on their individual sheets. Encourage class members to suggest titles for each day. At the end of the week, students can take these sheets home—and perhaps produce them in response to the question "What did you do in school?"

Taste Treat

Materials: Cabbage, mayonnaise, pineapple, carrots, raisins, large bowl, spoon, copies of recipe (see below)

Group size: Large group, whole class

Provide your students with copies of the following recipe as well as the appropriate ingredients:

3 cups shredded cabbage

⅔ cup mayonnaise

¼ cup crushed pineapple

¼ cup shredded carrots

¼ cup raisins

Blend mayonnaise and cabbage in a large bowl. Add pineapple, carrots, and raisins, and mix well.

Direct your students to prepare the recipe according to the directions. Then have pupils contribute appropriate titles for the recipe. Ask them to defend their titles with reference to the ingredients or the preparation procedure. After you have several titles, post a copy of the recipe (perhaps including a photo of the finished product) and the various titles on the bulletin board. At the end of the week, have the students vote for their favorite title. Post the winning title over the recipe and photo.

_____ **Adaptation** _____

Designate a day as recipe day. Encourage your students to work with their parents to prepare a favorite dish, treat, or dessert to bring into class on the designated day. These could then be displayed on a counter or table. Select a few of these, and ask the students to look them over carefully. Then ask the class for appropriate names. Cards could then be prepared and placed next to each designated item.

Recipe Roundup

Materials: No-bake recipes, ingredients, kitchen equipment
(see below)

Group size: Individual, small group

Bring in several simple recipes for no-bake cookies. Remove the
titles, and direct your pupils to prepare them according to the
directions. By adding nuts, candy bits, chocolate chips, or food
coloring, your students should be able to produce a variety of
mouth-watering creations. Then ask your students to provide
names for their concoctions (for example, Jonathan's Crumbly Nut
Cookies or Rebecca's Pink Coconut Delight).

Here is a recipe to get you started:

Combine ¼ cup honey, ¼ cup peanut butter, and ½ cup
confectioner's sugar. Form the mixture into half-inch balls, and
roll them in graham cracker crumbs. Makes twelve cookies.

——— **Adaptation** ———————————————————————

You may wish to prepare one recipe while the entire class
observes. Ask the class for possible titles. Then question
the class as to how the title would change if one
ingredient were added (e.g., colored sprinkles), if two
ingredients were added (e.g., nuts, green food coloring),
and so on. Ask the students which title they think is the
best, and then add the necessary ingredients to conform
to that selection. Make sure there is enough of the recipe
for all to share.

Hands On

Materials: Paper, pencils, scissors

Group size: Individual

Ask each student to trace an outline of his or her hand on a piece of paper and cut it out. Upon completing a story in the basal reader, discuss with the pupils several important facts from the story. Direct each student to select five facts from the story and write one on each finger and thumb of the outline. Have them write the main idea of the story on the palm area. Set up a bulletin board display entitled *I've Got a Hand on Reading* and display these paper hands.

_____ **Adaptation** _____

You may want to introduce this activity to younger pupils by drawing an outline of a person on the chalkboard. After completing a story in the basal text, ask students to suggest important details from the story that can be written on the figure's arms and legs. A class title can then be suggested for the head. Point out how all the body parts (details) are connected to the head (main idea).

Story Time

Materials: Tape recorder, blank tape

Group size: Individual, small group

Place a cassette player and blank tapes in a corner of your room, and ask students to create and record their own stories during their free time. Encourage them to use their imaginations. Students who have difficulty may want to record stories that have been written as part of a creative writing exercise, or recount part of a book they have read. Try to have each student record at least one story. Then ask the pupils, either individually or in small groups, to listen to these stories and to create titles for each of them. Include these titles with each tape so that students can locate favorite stories to hear again. You may even wish to organize a classroom story library.

_____ **Adaptation** _____

For younger readers or those experiencing some reading difficulty, you may wish to select several stories from the basal reader that have already been read. Record these on separate tapes. Ask students to listen to them and suggest titles. They may want to compare their titles with the originals. Be sure to discuss any differences.

In Twenty-five Words or Less

Materials: Telegram forms
Group size: Individual

First, obtain blank telegram forms from the telegraph office, or design your own. Then, when a student has finished reading a book, have him or her state the main idea in a telegram. Point out that since telegrams are charged by the word, your students need to be as concise as possible while still getting the message across. After your pupils have prepared several telegrams, you may wish to initiate a telegram service by sending these to another class, which, in turn, would send your class telegrams of favorite books. By posting these telegrams on the bulletin board, you may encourage your students to discover new and interesting books.

_____ **Adaptation** _____

You may wish to prepare your own telegrams for books students have read. Post these messages along with a selection of book jackets on the bulletin board. Direct students to match telegrams with the correct books. Brief annotations on popular children's books can be obtained from book catalogs. Cut out some of these, separate the titles and annotations, post them on the board, and ask students to match them (choose books with which students are familiar or that they have already read).

Nine Plus!

Materials: Poster board, index cards, box

Group size: Individual, small group

Divide a large sheet of poster board into nine equal sections, and write the names of recently read basal or library stories in each of the squares. Post this on the bulletin board. Prepare a set of index cards, some with the main idea of each story noted (one per card) and some with specific details from each story (one per card). Mix these cards, and place them in a box. Direct students, one at a time or in small groups, to choose a card, determine if it is a main idea, and (if it is) tack it on the proper story title listed on the poster. Encourage students to defend their choices and to note the differences between the main idea cards and the detail cards.

_____ **Adaptation** _____

Older students may wish to construct a card game variation of this activity. Three detail cards and one main idea card could be prepared for each story. These cards would then be shuffled and dealt to players, who would attempt to assemble them into books of four cards according to the rules for Fish. These books could then be placed on the appropriate square of the poster board.

Once upon a Time

Materials: Shoe boxes, pictures, glue, pipe cleaners, paint, brushes, construction paper

Group size: Individual, small group

Read several fables to your students, but omit the morals. Instead, ask your pupils to formulate the morals of the stories on their own. Afterwards, direct each student to create a shoe box diorama of his or her favorite fable. Using pictures, glue, pipe cleaners, and construction paper, each student can create a three-dimensional representation of the characters and events of a fable in a shoe box set on its side. Have the students write the fable's moral on a miniature banner and post it over the box.

——— **Adaptation** ———————————————————————

Ask pupils to select an incident that has occurred at school or in the community. After sufficient discussion, direct the class to provide a moral (or, if applicable, a title) for the event. As new incidents occur, ask pupils to keep a record of these for later reference.

And the Winner Is . . .

Materials: None
Group size: Whole class

After you have finished reading a short story to the students, ask them to suggest alternate titles for the selection. Have the students defend their titles by listing supporting details from the story. After you have several titles, post a copy of the story (minus the original title) and the new titles on the bulletin board. At the end of the week, have the students vote for their favorite title, and display the winning title over the story.

_____ **Adaptation** _____

Write the titles of several stories on the chalkboard. Read a selected story to the class, and ask them to identify the corresponding title. Discuss with them the reasons why the other titles may be inappropriate.

Ad It Up!

Materials: Cereal boxes, crayons, paper, glue
Group size: Individual

Provide each student with a cereal box, and direct him or her to make up a magazine advertisement for that brand. Instruct each student to cut the cereal name off the box and incorporate it in the ad. Ask students to describe important qualities such as texture, flavor, and appearance and to use a variety of colors in the illustrations. Remind pupils that a good advertisement should focus on a product's most outstanding features—in other words, the biggest reasons why someone should buy this product. You may wish to have your students advertise their products, so to speak, to other classes or in the school newspaper.

_____ **Adaptation** _____

Ask students to identify items in the room that could be advertised. For example, what qualities would one emphasize in an aquarium, a globe, or the teacher's desk? Depending upon the age or reading ability of your pupils, you may want to lead them in an oral discussion or have them prepare a more formalized advertisement.

All the News

Materials: Newspapers, markers, tagboard, shoe box

Group size: Individual, whole class

Prepare several newspaper headlines that use students' names (for example, *Bill Thompson Elected Governor, Marcia Green Wins Olympic Gold Medal, Greg Banner Accepts Presidential Award*). Place these headlines in a box. Ask the pupils to select one headline each and to write a brief story to go with it. When several students have finished their stories, assemble the stories into a class newspaper, and distribute it to other classes. Be sure to discuss the importance of the titles as signals for the content of each story.

_____ **Adaptation** _____

> Ask each student to develop a personal headline using his or her own name. Then have each student stand and relate a short story that matches the headline, dictate a story on tape, or write an appropriate story on paper.

Mobile Mania

Materials: Magazines, scissors, tagboard, glue, coat hangers, string

Group size: Individual, small group

Have the students create main idea mobiles using popular subjects (e.g., baseball). Ask them to cut out pictures from old magazines that depict various aspects of that topic (for example, pitcher, umpire, baseball diamond). Direct the students to paste these pictures on pieces of tagboard and to tie them to a coat hanger. Have each pupil make a banner with the mobile's topic on it and affix the banner to the top of the mobile. These mobiles can then be displayed throughout the room and changed at regular intervals.

_____ **Adaptation** _____

Hang a picture of the entire class from a coat hanger. Ask pupils to suggest descriptive words, phrases, or sentences that can be written on slips of paper and hung under the photo. (This would make an interesting display for open house, meet-the-teachers night, etc.)

A Class Act

Materials: None

Group size: Large group, whole class

The use of pantomime is an excellent nonverbal way to communicate the importance of the main idea as a summarization process. Begin this activity by pantomiming several actions for your class, and direct the pupils to contribute titles for your actions. After you have mimed two or three, ask other class members to pantomime their own stories. The following suggested themes may help to get you started:

1. Driving a race car.

2. Planting flowers.

3. Playing football.

_____ **Adaptation** _____

For younger students, you may wish to write the titles of three or four favorite stories or books on the chalkboard. You can then pantomime the actions from one of the stories and ask pupils to match the actions with the appropriate title. Students may want to perform their own scenes in small groups, asking the rest of the class to make the appropriate matches.

2

Understanding Sequence

   Understanding the order of events in a story or reading selection is an important comprehension skill. It can also be a frustrating process for many children. Anyone who has attempted to get students to put five or six story events in the right order realizes the difficulties that some pupils have with this skill. Youngsters often tend to deal only with the here and now; a given event in the past can easily have happened last week or last year, as far as they are concerned.

   Teachers who use a variety of timely activities, based on students' own experiences, can help their pupils understand that sequencing is a part of everyday life. In fact, the skill of sequencing is best learned if it is presented as a logical component of your pupils' own lives. Daily activities such as preparing recipes, running errands, or even setting the dinner table all involve a necessary

order of events. Personalized activities, drawn from students'
experiences and incorporated into the instructional plan, help pupils
understand the process of sequencing. In addition, children begin to
understand *why* story events occur in a certain order. Most
important, children begin to realize that understanding order and
comprehending time are daily living skills just as they are essential
reading skills.

Seed-quencing

Materials: Radish seeds, clear plastic drinking cups, potting soil, paper and pencils, crayons

Group size: Individual

Direct each of your students to fill a plastic cup with potting soil. Have the children plant three or four radish seeds about one-half inch below the surface around the inside of the cup (this allows them to see the roots grow). Have them sprinkle water on the soil and place the cups in the window where they will receive sunlight.

Ask each student to draw an illustration of his or her cup and, under it, to write a short description of what he or she sees. Tell students to water their seeds every two or three days. Have them draw additional pictures of their seed cups every six days with a description of how the cups look at those times.

Have your pupils make a sequence booklet of their drawings and writings and place them on the bulletin board for others to see. At the end of the growing period (usually twenty-four to twenty-seven days for most varieties of radishes), permit your students to eat their radishes and share their booklets.

_____ Adaptation _____

There are a variety of filmstrips available that depict the growth of various plants. Obtain one of these and show it to your class. Stop the filmstrip every couple of frames and ask the class to describe the process (the steps can then be recorded on the chalkboard). Be sure to follow up with a discussion on why plants must follow a certain sequence in their growth cycle.

One Thing after Another

Materials: Index cards, pencils

Group size: Individual

Direct each of your students to take five index cards. On the front of each card have pupils write down something that they do almost every day (for example: wake up, go to school, eat lunch). Have them number the back of each card in the proper sequence. Tell them to mix the cards and have a classmate put them in the right order. Classmates can check the answers by turning the cards over to see if they read 1, 2, 3, 4, 5.

_____ **Adaptation** _____

For younger pupils, you can reduce the number of cards used from five to three, ask them to draw pictures instead of writing phrases or sentences, or reduce the number of cards to two and have pupils record things done at the beginning of the day as well as things done at the end of the day.

Order, Order

Materials: Paper and pencils, scissors, checkerboard, checkers

Group size: Individual

Ask each of your students to write out the directions for playing a game of checkers. Tell them to cut out each sentence and then mix the sentences. Direct each student to pass the sentences to a friend, who can then put the sentences in the right order. When the friend is finished, the two students can check the work by playing a game of checkers according to the order of the directions.

Provide some variety by asking your students for suggestions as to other games that require a specified order of steps. Have the students use this activity with other popular table games.

_____ **Adaptation** _____

You may wish to have groups of younger students make up directions for locating another room in the school, locating a specific item in the classroom, or getting from school to a park or playground. These directions could be written or dictated, depending on the age or abilities of your class.

This Is Your Life

Materials: Index cards, crayons, clothespins, string, thumbtacks
Group size: Individual

Ask your students each to take five index cards. Direct each to
draw pictures on separate cards of things that have happened in his
or her life (for example, birth, first day at school, getting braces).
Have them write a title for each picture. Tell them to put two
thumbtacks in the bulletin board about five feet apart and tie a
piece of string between the thumbtacks. Using clothespins, have
them attach their pictures to the string in the correct order.

_____ Adaptation _____

Ask students to select a significant event for each day
over the course of a week. These can be recorded on
individual index cards. At the end of the week, tape
these cards in random order to the chalkboard, and ask
students to place them in proper sequence. This activity
can also be done by selecting a few events of a certain
day. The cards could then be manipulated at the end of
each day.

Pocket It!

Materials: Several old pairs of jeans, index cards, tape recorder, blank tape

Group size: Individual, small group

Set up a bulletin board display by posting a pair of denim jeans (or just the rear pocket area) up on the board. Label one pocket *beginning*; the other, *end*. Select a story and record it on cassette tape. Prior to introducing it to your students, write several events that occur at the beginning of the story and several that occur at the end on index cards. Direct your pupils to listen to the story. Then have them sort through the cards, placing them in the correct pocket on the bulletin board.

You can expand this activity by sewing three or four pockets to a piece of fabric, numbering the pockets, and asking pupils to place sequence cards into the proper pockets.

_____ **Adaptation** _____

An easier version of this activity would be to record a variety of events from a selected story randomly on the chalkboard. After students have finished reading the story, ask the class to group these events into two (beginning, end) or three (beginning, middle, end) categories. Be sure the class has an opportunity to reach a consensus of opinion on the correct placement.

Your Order, Please

Materials: For each group: ¾ cup ground dried apricots, 1 cup shredded coconut, ⅓ cup condensed milk, confectioner's sugar, mixing bowl, waxed paper, instruction sheet

Group size: Small group, large group

Prepare instruction sheets with the recipe for apricot-coconut balls, below. As you can see, the order of the directions is scrambled. Instruct each group to discuss the proper arrangement of directions and to designate one person to write the directions in the right order. Then each group can make a batch of these cookies in accordance with its directions. Provide each group an opportunity to discuss its recipe with others.

Apricot-Coconut Balls

Next, roll the balls in sugar.

First, combine the apricots and coconut.

Last, place the balls on waxed paper to dry for one hour.

Then add milk to the apricot-coconut combination and mix well.

After mixing, shape the mixture into one-inch balls.

_____ Adaptation _____

Provide your students with copies of old cookbooks or photocopies of several recipes (there are many excellent cookbooks available for kids). Work with them in locating words such as *after*, *then*, or *next* that identify a particular sequence of instructions. The class may then want to make up a list of these words. Discuss with them the possibilities for using these words in other activities (building models, making a bed, etc.).

Follow That Tune

Materials: Tape player, recorded tape, worksheets (see below)

Group size: Individual, small group, large group, whole class

Choose three or four sentences from a popular song, and write them out of order on a worksheet. Instruct your students to review the sentences, listen to the song on the tape player, and then stop the player. Next, ask them to number the sentences in the order in which they occur in the song. Have them put a 1 in front of the sentence that came first, a 2 in front of the second, and so on. When they are through, have them rewind the tape and check their work. Encourage groups to use new songs to make up their own worksheets for exchange.

_____ **Adaptation** _____

For a simpler activity, write nursery rhymes on the chalkboard, but mix up the order of the lines. Direct the class to rearrange each rhyme into its correct sequence. You may even wish to write individual lines on separate strips of paper, thus giving your pupils an opportunity to manipulate the respective lines.

Saturday Morning Sequence

Materials: A Saturday morning TV listing, worksheet (see below)

Group size: Individual

Make up a sequence worksheet based upon popular shows shown on television on Saturday morning. On the worksheet, ask students to do one of the following: (1) rearrange several show titles in the order of their appearance in the listing, (2) write the times that particular programs come on, or (3) check the schedule to determine which shows come on either before or after a specific program.

You may also want to have students develop their own worksheets to be completed by other members of the class. These worksheets could be distributed on Friday afternoon as a prelude to the Saturday shows.

_____ **Adaptation** _____

Provide each student with a blank index card, and direct him or her to write the name of a favorite TV show or program. Collect the cards, and tape them to the chalkboard (try to avoid duplications). Work with the class in assembling the shows in the order in which they are televised, by day of the week, and then by time of day if you wish. You may choose to duplicate the list and have pupils work in small groups to put the titles in the correct sequence.

Scenes in Sequence

Materials: Cardboard boxes, paper, dowels, tape, crayons, paint

Group size: Individual, small group

Direct your pupils to cut a six-inch by six-inch square hole in the center of each box bottom. With the cutout facing them, have them cut four small holes in what are now the top and bottom of the box, two across from each other to the right of the cutout and two across from each other to the left of the cutout. Show them that dowels can be inserted in these holes. Demonstrate that each box can now form a TV set with a screen and a place to wind a picture scroll.

Ask each student to choose five events from his or her favorite story and to draw a picture representing each event on one sheet of paper. Have each pupil then tape the papers together so that the events are in the proper order from left to right. Tell them to tape a blank sheet of paper on each end. Have them place a dowel through the holes in the right side of the box (with the cutout section facing them). Have them tape the sheet of paper that is on the end of each story to that dowel and wind it up counterclockwise. Have them place the other dowel in the holes in the left side of each box. Direct them to tape the sheet of paper that is at the beginning of their story on that dowel. Direct them to twist the left-hand dowel clockwise to wind the paper past the window. Have them tell their individual stories to a friend as he or she watches the show.

_____ **Adaptation** _____

You may be able to obtain several old or discarded filmstrips. Cut these apart into three or four sections. Ask groups of students to splice the pieces of each filmstrip together in the correct order (using transparent tape) to show to the rest of the class.

There are also blank filmstrip kits available commercially with which pupils can create their own individual filmstrip programs.

The Word Series

Materials: Small milk cartons, paper

Group size: Individual

Print several sentences on strips of paper. Cut each strip apart between the words, number the words on the back to reflect their original order in the sentence, and place each cut-up sentence in a carton (these can be decorated). Direct each student to take the words out of one carton and lay them down on a table or desk. Have each pupil rearrange the words so that they make a complete and understandable sentence. Students can check their answers by looking at the number on the back of each word. Give your students the opportunity to create their own sentence strips to share with their friends as well.

_____ **Adaptation** _____

For younger students, you may want to use appropriate spelling words in one of the following ways:

1. Write words on the chalkboard but mix up the order of the letters. Ask the class to rewrite the letters in the right order.

2. Choose a vocabulary word and write it with one letter to a card. Students can then rearrange the letters into the right sequence.

3. Give students a selection of cards, each with a letter, and have them compose appropriate words.

Growing and Showing

Materials: Student-selected photos, scrapbook materials (see below)

Group size: Individual

Ask your students to bring in several photographs of themselves taken at various times in their lives (four or five each should be sufficient). Direct them each to assemble these photos into a scrapbook (several sheets of construction paper stapled together with tagboard covers) and to provide a brief caption for each photo. Discuss with your pupils the reasons why their photos were placed in a particular order. Relate the sequence of their individual time lines to the sequence of events in a popular story. Be sure students have an opportunity to share or display their scrapbooks.

_____ **Adaptation** _____

Younger students may wish to draw three different pictures, each depicting a particular stage or event in their lives. A one- or two-sentence caption for each picture should also be supplied. These can then be displayed on the bulletin board or in a special corner of the room.

Picture Perfect

Materials: Tape player, blank tape, story cut from an old picture book (including at least four illustrations)

Group size: Small group, large group

Beforehand, record yourself reading the story. Cut out the illustrations, and number them in order on the back. Direct your students to listen carefully to the story. After the story is over, have them put the pictures in correct order according to the sequence of events in the story. Students can check their answers by turning the pictures over and referring to the numbers on the back, or by listening to the story again.

―――― **Adaptation** ―――――――――――――――――――――――――――――

Select several cartoons from the daily or Sunday newspaper. Paste each on stiff cardboard, and cut apart the panels. Put numbers on the back of each panel. Place each set in an envelope. Direct students to select an envelope and arrange the cartoon strip in the proper order. Students can check their answers by turning over the cards and observing the order of the numbers.

Yum-Yum

Materials: Bananas, pineapple, fruit cocktail, small marshmallows, sour cream, bowl, spoon, copies of recipe (see below)

Group size: Small group, large group

Provide students with copies of the following recipe as well as the appropriate ingredients:

1 cup sliced bananas

1 cup crushed pineapple

1 cup fruit cocktail

1 cup tiny marshmallows

1 cup sour cream

Direct groups of students to create sets of directions for preparing this recipe. Instruct them to preface each directional statement with a word such as *first*, *after*, *then*, *next*, or *last*. Distribute these directions to other groups of students, and ask them to prepare the recipe in accordance with the specific instructions.

―――― **Adaptation** ――――――――――――――――――――

Prepare the recipe for the entire class (perhaps doubling or tripling the amounts). Have students suggest a possible order of preparation, which can be recorded on the chalkboard by individual pupils. Encourage students to utilize the prefacing words mentioned above and to place numbers in front of each direction.

Day by Day

Materials: Chalk, chalkboard
Group size: Whole class

On the chalkboard, make up a time chart that lists each hour of the typical school day. Ask your pupils to list, in order, the various events that occur on a normal day. Discuss with them the reasons why these events occur in the order that they do. Would the schedule be upset if some or all of the events were placed at different times or rearranged?

Have each student make a time chart of his or her typical weekend day at home. Ask them to compare school days with weekends. You may want to display these charts in the classroom or gather them together to make a time book.

_____ **Adaptation** _____

You may wish to bring in bus, train, or airplane schedules to display for the class. Discuss with your students the reasons why these forms of transportation must adhere to such rigid schedules. What are the potential consequences if the schedules are not followed? Some pupils may want to make up a transportation schedule for their own households that could be used for classroom display.

Stuck-up!

Materials: Popsicle sticks, magnets, glue

Group size: Individual, whole class

Prior to introducing a story in the basal reader to your students, take several Popsicle sticks and write down one important story event on each. Glue a small magnet on the back of each stick and randomly place them on a magnetic chalkboard or other appropriate surface. As you discuss the story, ask pupils to come up and arrange the sticks in the proper story sequence.

A variation would be to write the numbers 1, 2, and 3 on the board and ask students to place some sticks under the 1 (events in the beginning of the story), 2 (events in the middle), or 3 (events at the end). Initiate a class discussion, and have pupils defend their stick placements.

—————— **Adaptation** ——————————————————————————

Ask students to write down particular story events on slips of paper. Have several students each randomly select a paper strip and note what is written on it. Have students with beginning events stand on one side of the room, those with medial events in the middle of the room, and those with ending events on the far side of the room. Make sure students have opportunities to defend their individual placements.

16

Part and Parcel

Materials: Large pictures, poster board, large envelope, chalk, chalkboard

Group size: Whole class and individual

Display a large picture for the class to see. Ask them to tell a story about the picture as a group while you write it on the chalkboard. When the story is completed, transfer the story to a large sheet of poster board. Cut the story into groups of sentences, and mix them up. Put the pieces into a large envelope, making sure there are numbers on the back of each section. Ask students to rearrange the story parts into the correct order. They can check the work by turning the pieces over. When everyone has had an opportunity to rearrange the story, post it in the room.

___ **Adaptation** _____

Obtain several old workbooks, and ask pupils to cut out a selection of stories. Each story can then be divided into three or four parts, mixed up, and placed in an envelope. Other pupils can then piece these stories together. They may then wish to provide an appropriate illustration or drawing.

Now Appearing

Materials: Paper and pencils

Group size: Whole class

Ask someone to walk into your classroom at a specified time, perform four or five actions, and then leave. Then have the students write down everything the person did, and in the correct order. Put together a group story about the incident, and post it on the bulletin board. Be sure that everyone agrees on the proper order of events.

Example: Samuel walks in.

1. He sits in a chair.

2. He ties his shoelaces.

3. He raises a pencil over his head.

4. He points to the clock.

5. He stands up on one leg.

He leaves the room.

_____ Adaptation _____

After your students have watched a film, movie, or filmstrip, ask them to name some of the events depicted and list them in the proper order on the chalkboard. Or you may wish to provide the class with a list of preselected events that can be sequenced. You may want to have younger pupils talk about the events rather than record them on the chalkboard.

One More Part

Materials: Picture cards
Group size: Whole class

Prior to reading a story to the class, make up four or five picture cards illustrating various events in the story. Show the cards to the class, and then read the story. After finishing the story, remove one of the cards, and put the remainder on the chalk tray of the chalkboard. Ask the class to review the remaining scenes and to tell you the missing card. Question them as to why that scene was important to the story, if it could be put in another place, or if it could be eliminated. Prepare other picture cards for future stories in the basal text.

___ Adaptation _____

After reading several stories, you may want to have small groups of pupils make up their own sets of picture cards. These sets could then be displayed to the class. Class discussions would focus on matching each set of cards with its appropriate story. Provide each group with an opportunity to share its reasons for selecting the story events portrayed.

3

Grasping Details

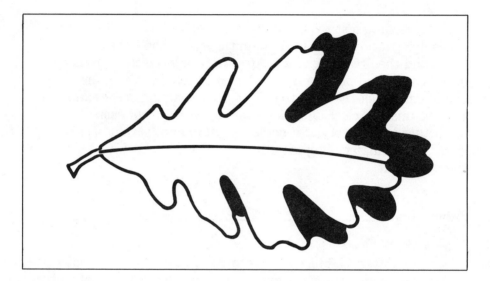

Details are the essential facts or data of a story upon which all the action is based. Understanding the specifics of characters, settings, or events in a story is important to a reader's overall comprehension. In good expository writing, details have a relationship to one another, thus laying a foundation for higher-level comprehension skills.

Students need to be able to sort through the mass of details present in a story and determine whether each one is important or unimportant to the rest of the story, and whether each one can be compared with other facts evident in the story. Being able to recognize and remember story details is a valuable reading skill, one that relies on both visual and auditory memory cues to recall significant data.

Students deal with details every day, from the food they eat for breakfast and the subjects they study in school to the TV programs they watch at home. Building up an awareness of how details are related (i.e., categorized) will help students understand the relevance of details in written material as well as assist them in remembering important facts.

Character Cards

Materials: Tagboard, markers
Group size: Small group, large group

Cut up several sheets of tagboard into playing-card-size pieces. Prior to reading a story to your class, make up four character cards for each character in the story by printing one fact about a character per card. Shuffle all the cards.

Read the story to your class (or make a tape recording beforehand for small groups of pupils to hear on their own). Upon completion of the story, have groups of students play Character Match (use the rules for Fish). The object of the game is to obtain as many pairs as possible. Each of the cards in a pair must have a detail pertaining to the same character, and the player must properly identify the character. The person with the most matches wins the game.

You may also wish to create separate decks of cards for settings, events, or times within a story.

_____ **Adaptation** _____

Students may wish to draw silhouettes of selected characters from a story. Each pupil can then list several facts about a character within the appropriate silhouette. These can then be cut out and displayed in the room under the matching story titles. They may also be collected into a scrapbook that could be set up for all to see.

Snap, Crackle, Pop

Materials: Cereal boxes, index cards, cardboard box
Group size: Individual

Using index cards, write down some details from several different brands of breakfast cereal (e.g., ingredients, key words, special offers). Mix up the cards, and place them in a brightly colored box. Set up a variety of cereal boxes on a counter or desk. Have students sort through the index cards and place them in the boxes of the corresponding brands of cereal. Ask students to make up their own cards for others to match to specific cereal boxes.

_____ **Adaptation** _____

Younger students may each wish to list four or five specific details about themselves on individual index cards. These cards could then be displayed on each pupil's desk, in an appropriate display on the bulletin board, or in a class scrapbook. Later you may want to randomly select several cards, read them to the class, and ask pupils to identify the specific individuals to whom the cards refer.

Word Whirl

Materials: Prepared worksheet (see below)

Group size: Individual, small group, large group, whole class

Prepare a word search puzzle using the specific details of a story. Provide a variety of examples of characters, settings, scenes, and actions within the puzzle. After your students have read the story, ask them to locate specific details of the story within the puzzle. After some practice, your pupils may want to create their own puzzles for their classmates or friends, using either library books or stories from the basal reader.

The following example uses words found in *Curious George Gets a Medal* by H.A. Rey (Boston: Houghton Mifflin Co., 1957).

										Word bank	
P	I	G	S	T	C	M	L	F	M	cow	pigs
E	Y	E	L	L	O	W	H	A	T	pen	pump
N	A	O	D	H	W	F	I	R	N	lather	ink
C	U	R	I	O	U	S	N	M	P	medal	soap
B	C	G	L	S	H	O	K	E	U	farmer	yellow hat
G	K	E	M	E	D	A	L	R	M	George	hose
L	A	T	H	E	R	P	E	J	P	curious	

Note: Words go across or down.

Adaptation

Develop this activity as a whole class or small group experience by asking students for specific story details that can be recorded on the chalkboard. Separate groups can then be charged with the responsibility of making their own puzzles using selected words from the class list. These puzzles can then be exchanged between groups.

Ten Questions

Materials: Photograph or picture
Group size: Small group, large group

Show a large picture or photograph to the class for one minute. Ask each member to observe the details of the picture very carefully. After one minute, remove the picture and organize the class into several groups. Each group is then responsible for writing ten questions, the answer to each being a detail from the picture. Give each group an opportunity to ask another group its questions. Make sure that each group has an opportunity to ask and answer different questions. Afterwards, show the picture again to the class so that all may recheck their answers (and questions).

___ **Adaptation** _____

One variation would be to have the class look at a specified picture for one minute. After its removal, have students list as many details as possible on the chalkboard. Then show the picture again so that responses can be checked.

Another adaptation would be to supply the class with a prepared question, the answer to which is a detail from a picture. Show the picture for one minute and ask the class to locate the detail that is the answer.

Room-mates

Materials: Sheets of poster board, magazines, scissors, glue
Group size: Small group, large group

On each of several sheets of poster board, draw an outline of a house (looking down into the interior). Include rooms such as the living room, dining room, kitchen, bedrooms, bathroom, and den. Give each group one of the sheets and a collection of old magazines. Instruct your pupils to cut out pictures of items that specifically belong in the rooms of the house (for example, toothpaste—bathroom, couch—living room, cheese—kitchen). Ask each group to glue its items in the proper rooms on the poster board. Later you may want to display these posters in the classroom.

A follow-up activity might include a class discussion of why some items belong in specific rooms just as some details are specific to certain stories.

―――― **Adaptation** ――――――――――――――――――――

Direct small groups of students each to choose a particular room in a house and locate pictures of items that belong in that room. Each group would then be responsible for assembling a collage on that room. These collages could then be shown to other groups or displayed.

Two Heads Are Better

Materials: Art materials (paint, brushes, tagboard, crayons), writing material (paper and pencils), scissors

Group size: Small group

After your students have finished reading a story in the basal text, divide the class into teams of two students each, instructing each team to prepare a character book. One person on the team will be responsible for drawing or sketching an illustration of a particular story character. The other person on the team will write a description of the character, which will include all of the essential details. This work can then be assembled into a book as follows:

1. Cut out the picture of the character. This becomes the book cover.

2. Place the cover on several sheets of writing paper, and cut around the outline.

3. The student author then writes the character description on the paper.

4. Bind the pages together with tape or staples. Put all character books out for display.

_____ **Adaptation** _____

Draw outlines of two or three characters from a selected story on the chalkboard. Ask class members to contribute specific details about each character. These facts can then be written inside each outline. Lead a discussion on any similarities or differences that exist between characters.

Beanbag Bonanza

Materials: Soft-drink bottle case (wood, with twenty-four compartments), tagboard, beanbags, markers, paint

Group size: Large group

Obtain a soft-drink bottle case, and repaint it in bright colors. Prepare tagboard cards the size of each compartment. On the front of each card, write the title of a popular story or children's book. On the reverse, write a number from one to three. Place a card (with the title side up) in each of the twenty-four compartments. Then play the game in the following manner:

1. Organize the class into two, three, or four teams.

2. Each team member stands back from the box a specified distance and tosses a beanbag into the case.

3. When a beanbag lands in a compartment, the student must provide two important details from that particular story. If the student answers correctly, his or her team gets the number of points on the back of the card; if incorrectly, the team loses that number of points.

4. The first team to reach a certain number of points (e.g., twenty-five) is declared the winner.

In order to keep the game interesting, state that no details may be used more than once for any single story.

—————— **Adaptation** ——————————————————————————

This game can also be played on the chalkboard by drawing a chart with twenty-four squares. Write the name of a story in each square and a number in the upper right-hand corner of each square. Cover each square with a piece of paper taped to the board. Individual team members then select a square, lift the paper, and identify two details for the story listed. The game can be scored as in the example above.

Leaves, Please!

Materials: Green construction paper, tree outline (see below), book covers, box

Group size: Individual, whole class

Cut a large outline of a tree from brown wrapping paper, and post it on the bulletin board. On the ends of four or five branches, tack a book cover (or a photocopy of a book cover) of a story you have read to the class or one that several pupils may have read independently. Cut out a number of leaves from the construction paper, and place them in a box. Direct your pupils each to take several leaves and to write a detail from one of the posted books on each leaf. Then students can tack their leaves on the branches holding the appropriate books. Students may wish to make their own individual trees for other books read during the year.

_____ **Adaptation** _____

Your students may wish to construct a class mobile. Attach a book cover to a coat hanger, and tie several pieces of string or yarn to the hanger. Individuals or groups of pupils can contribute index cards upon which have been written several details from the story. These cards could then be tied to the strings. A variety of drawings or illustrations could also be used for individual cards on the mobile.

Radio Roundup

Materials: Radio, paper, pencils
Group size: Whole class

Ask your class to listen to the radio for a specified length of time (for example, two minutes). As they listen, have them write down all the important details they hear (names of songs, public service announcements, commercials, etc.). You should prepare your own list, too. At the end of the time period, compare your pupils' lists with your own. Discuss what makes a particular detail important or unimportant.

You may wish to have your students focus on one particular type of presentation (for instance, commercials, music) and note specific types of details. Recording the selection for playback later may help in recalling and checking details.

_____ **Adaptation** _____

Tell students that during a specified time of the day (between 10:35 and 10:40, for example) they are to record as many classroom sounds that occur in that time span as possible. Direct students to share their lists and to note similarities and differences.

Younger students may also want to listen for one specific sound (school bell, siren, pencil sharpener) and to notify you when it occurs.

Jumping Around

Materials: Checkerboard, checkers, paper strips, tape

Group size: Small group

On each black square of a checkerboard, tape a detail from one of four different stories that the class has read. Tell pupils that during free time they may play the game, but with one rule change: whenever a checker lands on a square, the player must identify the specific story that contains the detail. If a player cannot provide the required information, then he or she loses a turn.

Have students make up their own checkerboards for other stories read. Keep a detail file, and replace squares at regular intervals to keep games interesting.

_____ **Adaptation** _____

One possible adaptation would be to have students bring in discarded game boards from home. Groups of pupils could suggest story details that could be placed in appropriate squares, circles, or boxes on each board in accordance with the instructions above. You may even wish to divide the whole class into two separate teams to play selected games.

Cast a Shadow

Materials: Paper, pencils, strong light
Group size: Individual

Ask each student to sit sideways in front of a large sheet of paper. Shine a strong light or an overhead projector at the student's head to create a silhouette on the paper. Direct another student to draw around the outline. Provide individual silhouettes for each pupil in the room.

Then instruct each student to record within the silhouette outline specific details about his or her life, such as hobbies, pets, family members, and favorite TV shows. When completed, these silhouettes can be displayed around the room. Be sure to take some time to discuss the reasons why everyone's specific details are different, just as the details in various stories are different and yet help us understand the story better.

_____ **Adaptation** _____

Younger students may wish to trace animal outlines taken from picture cards or story illustrations. Within each tracing, individual pupils or groups may wish to record details or facts specific to the animal illustrated. These drawings could then be displayed in an appropriate place in the room.

Twenty Questions

Materials: None
Group size: Whole class

Select a story with which your class is familiar or that your class has read recently. Pick out a particular detail from the story (character, setting) and initiate a game of twenty questions as follows:

1. The object of the game is for students to guess the specific detail you have in mind by asking twenty or fewer questions.

2. They may ask any kind of question as long as it can be answered yes or no.

3. The student who correctly guesses the detail may then be the leader, picking out another detail for the class to guess.

Vary the game by having the class determine the selected fact in ten questions or fewer.

―――― Adaptation ――――――――――――――――――――――――――

You may wish to vary this activity by asking students to select a specific feature of the room to identify in twenty questions or fewer. Other possible subjects include individuals within the school, other rooms, or particular items that students are wearing.

Younger players may enjoy this activity by attempting to identify a specific feature in a picture accompanying a particular story.

Mix and Match

Materials: Strips of tagboard, box

Group size: Individual, small group

Choose several stories that the class will be reading in the near future, and select five to seven details from each one. Write each of these facts on separate strips of tagboard. Create a bulletin board display with the titles of these stories at the tops of columns on the board. Place all the detail strips in a colorful box near the display. When your students have read a story, ask them to go through the box, choosing the details specific to the reading selection. Have them post the strips under the title of the corresponding book or story. Your students may want to create additional strips for other facts found in each story.

_____ Adaptation _____

You can initiate a detail-of-the-day display. Choose a specific detail from a recently read story, and write it on the chalkboard. Provide opportunities for individuals to discuss the detail and to arrive at a consensus on the name of the corresponding story, which can be written alongside. Depending on the age or ability of your students, you may want to go back to stories read a few days or weeks ago to select the details.

Sing Along With . . .

Materials: Prerecorded songs

Group size: Large group, whole class

Using the details from one specific story and the music from any popular children's song, turn a story into a song. Work with students in selecting not only the most important details but a tune with which they are familiar ("Happy Birthday," "For He's a Jolly Good Fellow"), one that appeals to the class. After some practice, your students will find this process both exciting and easy.

Later on, you may want to have the students choose tunes that are currently popular on the radio. Also consider recording these songs to share with other classes. By working with another teacher, you may be able to put together a basal text concert for a grade level lower than yours as a prelude to the stories that those students will encounter next year.

___ **Adaptation** _____

Obtain a recording of a popular children's song. Prior to playing it for the class, direct students to record details that they feel are important to the song. Then play the song so that answers can be checked. You may also wish to have students listen to several songs, list a variety of details, and then arrange them under appropriate titles.

Like a Bowlful of Jelly

Materials: Grape juice, sugar, pectin, bowl, spoon, glass jars, art
materials, glue, poster board

Group size: Large group, whole class

Provide groups of students with copies of the following recipe and
the proper ingredients:

3 cups Concord grape juice

5 cups sugar

4 ounces pectin (½ bottle)

Mix the juice and sugar and allow to stand for ten minutes. Add
the pectin and stir for three minutes. Pour into jars and cover.
Let stand for twenty-four hours. Makes about 5 cups of
grape jelly.

After you have prepared the recipe with your students, ask
them to draw separate pictures of each of the ingredients. Also
direct them to draw a picture of the final product. Have them glue
the three ingredient pictures on a piece of poster board along with
the illustration of the finished product. Ask them to put plus signs
between the first and second and between the second and third
ingredient pictures. Have them put an equal sign between the third
ingredient and the illustration of the finished product. Display
these murals in the classroom.

Adaptation

If possible, obtain old cookbooks that contain photos or
illustrations of the preparation of certain recipes. Direct
students to cut out necessary pictures of a specific recipe
and arrange them into a mural or scrapbook. Students
may also wish to draw illustrations of the ingredients of
a certain recipe and then arrange them in an equation, as
in the grape jelly example above.

And Now Presenting . . .

Materials: Paint, paper, crayons

Group size: Small group, large group

Discuss with your students several details from a story that the class has read together. Instruct groups of students to prepare a magazine advertisement for that selection in order to try, as it were, to sell the story to another class. Discuss with them the principles of a good ad (interest, appeal to the individual reader, emphasis on the benefits of the product, design). When the ads are completed, post them for others to see. As students advertise other stories, you may wish to gather them together for next year's class, which may find the ads to be an interesting prelude to the stories it will read.

You may want to give your pupils the option of selecting their own stories and choosing the specific details from each that they want to use in their ads.

___ **Adaptation** _____

Provide large groups of students with scissors, glue, construction paper, and old magazines. Direct them to leaf through several magazines and locate pictures of objects that have appeared in a recently read story. These pictures can then be cut out and assembled into a collage that can be displayed for the rest of the class or for the school.

Pick-up Sticks

Materials: Popsicle sticks

Group size: Small group

Provide your students with a quantity of Popsicle sticks. Ask each student to write one or more important details from a recently read basal story, one detail per stick. Mix the sticks, and provide several groups with an assortment of them. Direct each group to play a game of pick-up sticks with one unusual rule: before a stick can be claimed, the student selecting it must identify the story represented by the detail on the stick. Encourage pupils to create more detail sticks as other stories are read throughout the year.

_____ **Adaptation** _____

Ask students to come up to the chalkboard one at a time and write a detail from a story they enjoyed. When all details have been written, ask the class to categorize them according to story.

4

Drawing Inferences

Drawing inferences is a process of making educated guesses. Students need to understand that an author does not have to provide all the information necessary for a complete understanding of a story. Oftentimes, pupils must read between the lines, making conjectures and suppositions on the basis of a minimum of data.

There are two types of inference: deductive (going from the general to the specific) and inductive (going from the specific to the general). For example, when an author writes about a cold day, barren trees, and a snow-covered landscape, the reader should infer that the season is winter (by inductive reasoning). When a writer tells about a summer day, the reader may conjure up images of hot weather, ice cream trucks, and swimming pools (by deductive reasoning). Making inferences requires readers to have a sufficient

background of personal experiences as well as opportunities to take imaginative chances with their reading material.

Helping children with this comprehension skill requires patience and understanding on the part of the teacher. Teachers must be sensitive to the difficulty of the material presented as well as to the level of maturity of each student. However, when pupils understand that they make inferences every day—from deciding what to wear based on certain weather conditions to choosing particular TV programs—then this skill can also become a natural part of their reading development.

What's Inside?

Materials: Writing material, drawing material

Group size: Large group, whole class

You can help students make educated guesses by using picture books. Choose a popular picture book for children, but cover up the text with strips of paper. Show the pictures to the class, and ask the students to write a class story that would go with those illustrations. Compare their story to the original.

Another option is to select a picture book, but cover the illustrations with strips of paper. Read the book to the class and instruct students to draw illustrations that would match the text. Compare their pictures with those in the book.

Provide students with opportunities to display their work along with the actual books on the bulletin board.

_____ **Adaptation** _____

Select several wordless picture books, and show them to the class. If possible, use an opaque projector so that all students have an opportunity to see the pictures. Lead a discussion whereby commentary can be provided for each illustration in each book. You may wish to record some of these potential captions on the chalkboard.

Feelings

Materials: Photographs (see below), writing paper

Group size: Individual, small group

Display several photographs to the class, each illustrating a person with a particular emotion (happiness, sadness, anger). Direct your students to develop a short story that would go along with that emotion (what happened just prior to the photograph, during, or after?). Since students will have only a limited amount of information upon which to base their stories, be sure to give them some latitude in developing their creative writing. Be sure to post the pictures along with the stories on the bulletin board.

_____ Adaptation _____

Direct selected individuals to come to the front of the room and pantomime a preselected emotion. Ask class members to guess the emotion being demonstrated.

I've Got a Secret

Materials: Camera and film

Group size: Whole class

Take several photographs of various scenes and activities around
your school that children may not see often (superintendent
working, kitchen staff preparing lunch, custodian working on the
furnace). Post these photos on the bulletin board, and ask your
students to speculate on what may be happening in each picture.
Record their guesses; then take a field trip to observe and interview
these people firsthand. Have your pupils compare their original
guesses with their interview notes.

_____ **Adaptation** _____

Provide students with a partial description (either
written or oral) of some of the people who work in your
school or community. Ask pupils to speculate on who
these individuals may be.

Students should also be afforded opportunities to
offer partial descriptions so that other class members
may guess the identity of the mystery person.

4

Photo-Mate

Materials: Newspaper

Group size: Individual, small group

Cut out several photos from the newspaper. Have your students write stories that they think would be appropriate for those photographs. After everyone is finished, compare the actual stories with those created by your pupils. What features did they take for granted, which were left out, and which need further clarification? Post your students' stories and the news articles on the bulletin board.

_____ **Adaptation** _____

Obtain several old workbooks or storybooks, and cut out a selection of pictures. Show the pictures to the class, and have members relate a story that could go with each illustration or photo. Compare students' oral stories with those actually accompanying the pictures.

Close-ups

Materials: Camera and film

Group size: Individual, small group

You can provide practice in making inferences by photographing everyday objects in different ways. For example, close-up photographs of a butterfly's wing or a crack in a wall can be vehicles for making inferences about the larger objects. Common kitchen utensils, household implements, or classroom features, photographed up close or at an unusual angle, may appear to be something they are not. Display several examples of these photos for your class, and discuss features within each that may be familiar. Have pupils talk about the subject of each picture, and post their guesses next to each photo. Reveal the identity of the actual item in each photo at the end of the week.

_____ **Adaptation** _____

Select a picture from an old magazine, and cut it into two or three parts. Ask different groups of students to look at each part separately and make inferences as to what the rest of the picture may contain. Direct these groups to cooperate in putting their picture parts together and to compare their notes.

Show and Tell

Materials: Motion picture (see below) and projector
Group size: Whole class

Show a foreign language film to your class. At the conclusion of the movie, discuss with your pupils the possible conversations that people in the film may have been having. Talk about facial expressions, gestures, and body movements and how they may set the tone for the conversations. If there is a translation for the film, discuss it with your pupils.

If the film has English subtitles, block them out with a piece of cardboard as you show the movie. After the discussion, show the film again with subtitles, and compare students' perceptions of the conversations with those actually in the film.

_____ **Adaptation** _____

Direct groups of students to provide captions for individual frames of a selected filmstrip. If the filmstrip has captions, how do they compare with those of your students? If there are no captions for the filmstrip, can your students add theirs for showings to other classes?

Mystery Book

Materials: Dust jackets from several books

Group size: Individual

Obtain dust jackets from several books. Post them on the bulletin board, and ask your students to make some inferences about the characters, settings, and actions in each book. Post their guesses on the board, too. After reading each book to them, ask them for any modifications in their ideas. Discuss the similarities (or lack thereof) between the book cover and the book contents. Do the author's and cover artist's ideas match?

_____ **Adaptation** _____

Ask students to bring in several magazine pictures. Show these to the entire class, and tell them to suppose that each picture is an illustration from a particular book. Encourage class members to develop and dictate a story based on the illustration. You may wish to have them record the story on the chalkboard along with the picture.

Before and After

Materials: Newspaper or magazine pictures

Group size: Large group, whole class

From a newspaper or magazine, select a picture showing a lot of action (fire, auto race), and post it on the chalkboard. On the left side of the photo, write the word *before*; on the right side, write *after*. Have your students guess all the events that may have happened before or after that photo was taken, and record them on the board under the proper heading. Direct your pupils to defend their responses. Later you may wish to photocopy other pictures on worksheets (with *before* and *after* on them) and have pupils work in groups listing the possible events. These sheets could then be posted for display.

_____ Adaptation _____

Students may wish to bring in family photographs. Post a different photo each week on the bulletin board between two signs reading *before* and *after*. Ask class members to record possible events for each photo in the proper category. Provide variety by changing the photo each week.

Ask the student whose photo is being displayed to choose the information that most closely matches the actual events.

Square Off

Materials: Bingo sheets (see below), magazines, scissors, glue

Group size: Individual, small group

Prepare a bingo worksheet as follows: Divide a sheet of paper into sixteen squares. In each square, write a sentence such as the following:

We will go swimming tomorrow.

The planes are taking off.

The lion's roar scared me.

Preview the magazines beforehand so that you can compose sentences appropriate to the magazines' illustrations. Duplicate and distribute the sheets to your students. Direct them to look through the magazines to locate the scenes where those sentences could be spoken (for example, beach, airport, zoo). Have them cut out and paste pictures into each appropriate square on the sheet.

This activity could be extended by having pupils create their own worksheets for others to use.

_____ Adaptation _____

Select a list of places either in the school or around the local community, and list them on the chalkboard. Ask students to create dialogue that people in those locations may use (for example, "May I check out this book?" in a library).

Some students may wish to construct a scrapbook that includes photos or pictures of selected scenes and offer appropriate dialogue for each page.

Job Search

Materials: Index cards

Group size: Individual, whole class

Provide students with index cards, and ask them each to write down the tools, books, papers, implements, or other devices used in their mothers' or fathers' jobs. Post these cards around the room with a sheet of paper underneath each one. Encourage the students to guess the separate occupations represented by each group of tools. At the end of a week, have the class discuss each occupation and the items that are specific to it.

_____ **Adaptation** _____

You may wish to provide groups of pupils with a selection of pictures or words that belong to a specific category. Ask students to identify the particular topic. For example:

    tire, horn, gas, hood → car

    laces, heel, tongue, sole → shoe

11

Face-off

Materials: Camera, film

Group size: Small group

Go around the school and take photographs of children and adults demonstrating various emotions. You may need to stage certain shots. Provide small groups of students with one or two photos, and ask them to guess at the emotions displayed in each picture. Have them create a group story explaining what may have happened to cause each emotion. You may wish to have your pupils write their stories or record them on tape. Be sure to set up an appropriate place in the classroom to display these.

_____ **Adaptation** _____

To each of several groups of students, assign as a topic a specific emotion (e.g., happiness, anger, disgust), and ask each group to locate pictures in old magazines that seem to depict that feeling. Pupils may wish to make collages or mobiles illustrating the emotion assigned. Be sure to lead a class discussion in which you ask pupils to defend or explain their choice of pictures.

Greetings!

Materials: Several types of greeting cards, both traditional and contemporary

Group size: Individual

Cut the cover pages off several greeting cards. Distribute these cover pages to your students, and ask them to write or illustrate what they imagine might be an appropriate saying, quote, or humorous closing for the card. After several of these messages have been completed, give students the opportunity to compare their creations with the originals.

Keep these revised cards available throughout the school year for special or unusual occasions (birthdays, extended illnesses, upcoming vacations). These personalized cards will be well received by the members of the class.

_____ **Adaptation** _____

Obtain several old children's magazines. Remove stories from each, and cut off the endings. Bind each truncated story between sheets of construction paper and give it to a small group of students. Direct each group to create its own ending for the story and present it either orally or in writing to the rest of the class.

Sports Beat

Materials: Poster board, old magazines, glue, scissors

Group size: Small group, large group

Provide each group with an assortment of magazines, scissors, and glue. Have each group choose a popular sports figure, and instruct the pupils to cut out from the magazines pictures that might be associated with that particular person. For example, Wayne Gretzky might be illustrated by pictures of a hockey stick, a cheering crowd, ice, and money. Have students assemble these pictures into collages, which can then be displayed around the room.

One variation on this activity would be to assign a popular storybook character to each group as a collage subject.

_____ **Adaptation** _____

Record the names of various school personnel on the chalkboard. Ask class members to draw several pictures of items or events that they think would go with each person, each on a separate index card. Then tape the cards to the chalkboard next to the appropriate names.

A local celebrity or personality may also be an appropriate figure for this activity.

Radio Review

Materials: Prerecorded tapes (see below), tape player

Group size: Small group

Obtain several prerecorded tapes of old-time radio shows ("The Shadow," "Green Hornet," "Lone Ranger"). Rerecord them, but leave off the last two or three minutes of the show. Set up a tape player and the tapes in a corner of the classroom. Ask groups of students to listen to the rerecorded tapes and then to write what they think will happen at the end of the stories. Afterwards, you may want to play the entire stories for them so they can compare their predictions with the originals. You may want to keep a tally of whether or not students' predictions actually matched the contents of the stories—or if, indeed, they made the stories more exciting.

Students may also want to use this activity with upcoming stories in the basal text.

_____ **Adaptation** _____

At the beginning of each school day, read a selected story to your class, but leave off the ending. Sometime during the day, direct students to create possible endings either in writing or orally. At the end of the day, read the ending of the original story, and compare it with the students' versions. Be sure to discuss any similarities or differences.

Travel Time

Materials: Large assortment of travel brochures

Group size: Small group, large group

Obtain a large quantity of travel brochures from a travel agency. Cut off the covers and distribute them to various groups of students. Ask pupils to brainstorm as to what they would expect to find in each location or country. Make up a list for each brochure cover. Upon completion, ask pupils to compare their lists with the remainder of each brochure. What differences do they note, and what changes would they want to make in their lists?

_____ **Adaptation** _____

Brochures, pamphlets, and leaflets are available from a number of organizations and social agencies. Obtain a selection of these, and post them on a bulletin board. When students have free time, ask them to speculate on the contents of each brochure on the basis of the cover alone. Provide opportunities for students to compare their guesses with the actual contents.

Road Rally

Materials: Photos or illustrations of wordless traffic signs
Group size: Whole class

Present your students with examples of several common wordless traffic signs (merging traffic, no U-turn, divided highway). Ask them to guess at the meaning of each sign and to determine where they might find each one. Discuss with them why a particular design might have been chosen for a sign. You may want to have students design their own nonverbal traffic signs for specific conditions within their own neighborhoods (how would a warning for potholes look?).

_____ **Adaptation** _____

Rebus stories use pictures in place of certain words. Obtain several of these stories for your students, and work with them in deciphering some of the illustrations. Discuss the reasons why some words are easier to illustrate than others.

Students may wish to work together to create their own rebus stories.

Student Participation Charts

The student participation charts record the comprehension activities in which your pupils engage throughout the year. Each chart is headed by the name of the specific comprehension objective with a listing of each activity underneath. Across the top are spaces for student names.

Whenever a pupil participates in an activity, make a notation down from his or her name and across from the title of the specific activity as follows:

I—Individual

S—Small group

L—Large group

W—Whole class

Since the charts list all the available activities (space is provided for others you may wish to add), student completion of any activity or group of activities can be easily recorded. This procedure also permits teachers to group students for a specific activity in a rapid manner.

This information can then be used to determine student participation in any comprehension skill as well as provide a ready reference for administrators or parents.

Student Names

Getting the Main Idea

1 All Together Now								
2 Picture That								
3 Got a Match?								
4 The Place to Be								
5 Tune In								
6 Photo-Graphic Minds								
7 Class Calendar								
8 Taste Treat								
9 Recipe Roundup								
10 Hands On								
11 Story Time								
12 In Twenty-five Words or Less								
13 Nine Plus!								
14 Once Upon a Time								
15 And the Winner Is . . .								
16 Ad It Up!								
17 All the News								
18 Mobile Mania								
19 A Class Act								

	Student Names								

Understanding Sequence

1 Seed-quencing									
2 One Thing after Another									
3 Order, Order									
4 This Is Your Life									
5 Pocket It!									
6 Your Order, Please									
7 Follow That Tune									
8 Saturday Morning Sequence									
9 Scenes in Sequence									
10 The Word Series									
11 Growing and Showing									
12 Picture Perfect									
13 Yum-Yum									
14 Day by Day									
15 Stuck-Up!									
16 Part and Parcel									
17 Now Appearing									
18 One More Part									

	Student Names									

Grasping Details

1 Character Cards										
2 Snap, Crackle, Pop										
3 Word Whirl										
4 Ten Questions										
5 Room-mates										
6 Two Heads Are Better										
7 Beanbag Bonanza										
8 Leaves, Please!										
9 Radio Roundup										
10 Jumping Around										
11 Cast a Shadow										
12 Twenty Questions										
13 Mix and Match										
14 Sing Along With . . .										
15 Like a Bowlful of Jelly										
16 And Now Presenting . . .										
17 Pick-Up Sticks										

	Student Names								

Drawing Inferences

1 What's Inside?									
2 Feelings									
3 I've Got a Secret									
4 Photo-Mate									
5 Close-ups									
6 Show and Tell									
7 Mystery Book									
8 Before and After									
9 Square Off									
10 Job Search									
11 Face-off									
12 Greetings!									
13 Sports Beat									
14 Radio Review									
15 Travel Time									
16 Road Rally									